## ISLAND HERITAGE™
### P U B L I S H I N G
A DIVISION OF THE MADDEN CORPORATION

94-411 KŌʻAKI STREET, WAIPAHU, HAWAIʻI 96797
Orders: (800) 468-2800  •  Information: (808) 564-8800
Fax: (808) 564-8877
islandheritage.com

ISBN: 0-93154-839-X
First Edition, First Printing, 2005

Photography by Ron Dahlquist unless otherwise noted.

Designed by Angela Wu-Ki.

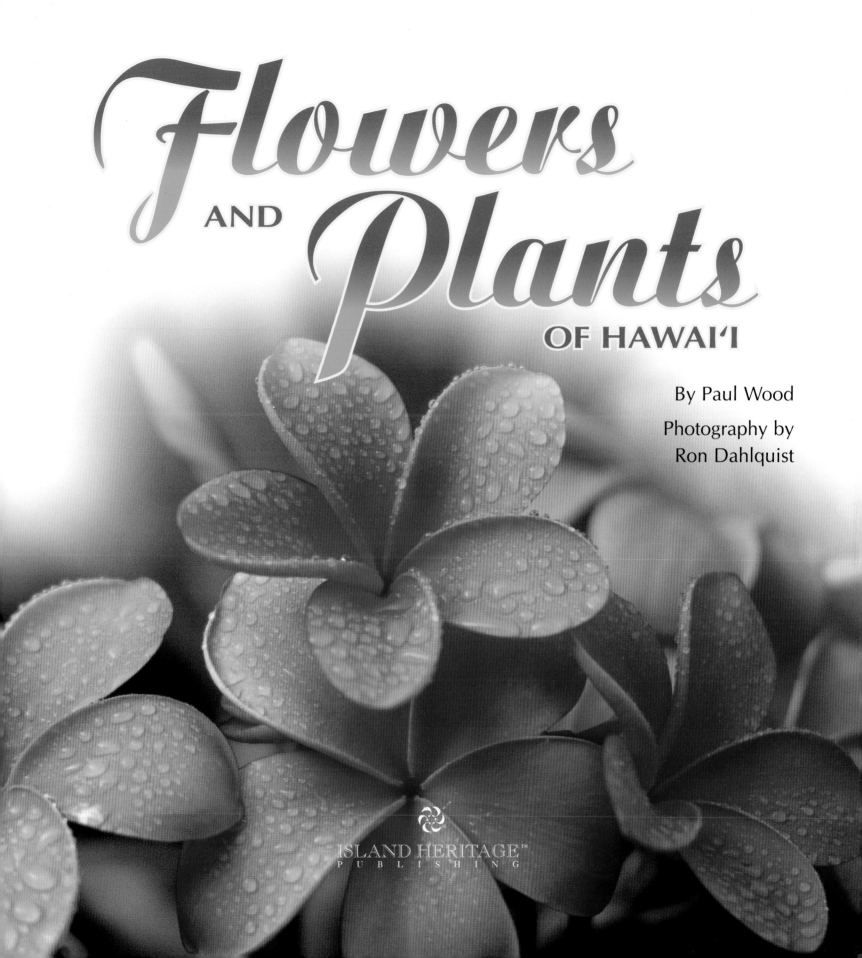

# Flowers
## AND
# Plants
## OF HAWAI'I

By Paul Wood

Photography by
Ron Dahlquist

ISLAND HERITAGE™
PUBLISHING

# Contents

# About This Book

"What's that flower?"
"What plant is that?"

The book you're holding right now is a "what's-that" book, designed to give ready answers to basic questions about Hawai'i's plants. It's for island visitors who have never been to the tropics and for island residents who never thought to ask.

It is not comprehensive, of course. A complete illustrated book showing all the plants that you're liable to see in Hawai'i, both in the wild and in the garden, would likely be large enough to stop traffic on Kalākaua Avenue. So I have chosen plants with the highest likelihood of eliciting questions from ordinary people.

I realize that my selection criterion is not very scientific. But let me hasten to add that I've made the answers as scientific as the book's size and your patience will allow. In each section, the plants are arranged alphabetically by their family name. That way, you can see that anthuriums are related to callas (of course!) and gardenias are related to coffee (how about that!). I hope this arrangement will give you a taste of the first pleasure in studying the natural sciences—the realization that the apparent chaos of life, when carefully observed, shows itself to be full of order and sense.

The major divisions of the book pay respect to the history of plants in Hawai'i. Section III, "Wild Ones," recognizes a few of the plants that had a strong presence in Hawai'i before the so-called discovery of the islands by Captain James Cook in 1778. Of course, because this is a "what's-that" book, I chose the ones you are likely to see—mai'a (banana) and maile, for example, but not the mulberry relative called wauke, which Hawaiians

grew in great quantity for the manufacture of kapa cloth but few gardeners cultivate today.

Section IV, "Roadside Plants," features plants that escaped from gardens and settled into the landscape, plants that you see on country drives and hiking trails, especially ones that are no longer cultivated much in gardens. I admit that this distinction is a bit forced. In Hawai'i many garden plants, especially vines, break loose and crowd the roadsides with displays that make drivers whip their heads around. If you can't find your drivers' distraction in section IV, flip through the picture index in the back of the book.

Sections V, VI, and VII divide garden plants by their habit of growth—soft stems, woody plants (that is, shrubs), and vines.

So what's missing? The trees! Hawai'i's magnificent trees, including the ones with showy flowers, are all collected in a companion pocket guide called *Tropical*

*Trees of Hawai'i*. You'll have to look there for the plumerias, the endemic 'ōhi'a, and most of the lavishly blooming members of the legume family.

Also, we deliberately omitted some of the most familiar garden plants, flowers that are not particularly unique to Hawai'i nor to tropical regions. These omitted plants include such globally popular species as the day lilies, irises, roses, nasturtiums, azaleas, and begonias, also certain landscaping stalwarts such as agapanthus and Natal plum.

You would think that the scientific names of plants are pretty well established. In fact, many have changed or are the subject of some controversy—botany is still a growing science. Whenever possible, I have leaned on authority of *Manual of Flowering Plants of Hawai'i*, a two-volume work by Wagner, Herbst, and Sohmer published by University of Hawai'i Press in 1960.

The paragraph provided with each plant answers more than the question "What's that?" In a compressed way, it tells a bit about how and where the plant grows, how it's used, and (if possible) how it got to Hawai'i. My highest hope is that this collection of stories will give you the pleasure of new understanding, also that it will give the world a desire to protect a certain delicate and unrepeated planetary jewel—the flora of the Hawaiian islands.

## PLANT FAMILY NAMES

When you start recognizing plant families, a sensible order begins to emerge from the blur of experience. Trouble is, the family names look so unfamiliar that they stun the mind. "Convolvulaceae," for example—if you can't pronounce it, how are you supposed to remember it?

But the names are easier than they first appear. All plant family names end in "aceae," which is always pronounced as though you are saying three letters in a row—A, C, E. Keep the emphasis on the "A," which is always the most accented sound in any family name.

This family tag "aceae" is attached to the name of the sub-group that botanists have chosen as the "type genus"—that is, the genus most typical of that family's fundamental approach to life. In the case of the Convolvulaceae—the viny, clinging morning-glory group—the type genus is called *Convolvulus*—which, if you think about it, is a good name for plants that twine, twist, and wind their way through life.

The rose family (type genus *Rosa*) is the Rosaceae. The daisy/sunflower family (type genus *Aster*) is the Asteraceae. Easy enough. Of course, you might choke a bit on Strelitziaceae and Zingiberaceae, families with a strong presence in this little guide. But give it a try. Family relationships are the key to the plant kingdom.

Finally, a word about our use of italics. Following standard practice, I have italicized every use of scientific names—that is, genus and species. When it came to the Hawaiian words, however, I applied a different standard. Strictly speaking, Hawaiian words are "foreign," so they should be italicized. But many Hawaiian plant names now stand as the accepted common name. Take maile, for example, which is the source plant for a popular lei.

Yes, "maile" is a Hawaiian word, but it is also a common household word (at least in the islands), equivalent to words like "petunia" and "pineapple." So "maile" has no more need of italics than do words like "lei" or "aloha." Rather than split hairs about which Hawaiian words are foreign, which are not, I chose to print them all in standard type. I hope this choice will not only provide clarity but also show my respect for the original name-givers of our native Polynesian plants.

# A Brief History of the Hawaiian Flora

From a plant's point of view, Hawai'i is impossibly far away. To find its way to Hawai'i on its own—by blowing, floating, or hitching a ride on a bird—a plant would have to cross at least twenty-five hundred miles of open sea.

That's a tough journey for any creature with roots. And yet, somehow, some plants did make the journey. By studying the native flora, botanists have made an educated guess at the number of individual species of flowering plants that managed to land, reproduce, and survive—less than 280. Over immense time, those unknown colonists adapted and developed into the total number of true native plants of Hawai'i, slightly less than a thousand.

As you can imagine, this native thousand is an unusual group—in fact, it is absolutely unique on Earth, and so it is a subject of both fascination and importance in the natural sciences. About 89 percent of them are endemic, not indigenous. In other words, the great majority are plants that occur nowhere in the world but Hawai'i.

The flora overall is odd in that so many of the world's plant families and types are absent—they never got to the islands. For example, despite the fact that the orchid family is the second largest on Earth, only three species of orchids are native to Hawai'i. Only one kind of palm tree made it. There is no native conifer—that enormous group of cone-bearing plants (pines, spruces, araucarias, and so on).

Of the 280 or so species that did make the trip, most (68 percent) were quite conservative—they found a niche, settled in, and stayed there, developing into one or two species. Few colonizers took advantage of the opportunity to radiate into many species. As a result, half of the native plant species arose from only 30 or so original colonizers (about 10 per-cent of them). One straggler that got to the islands, a member of a rather obscure family called Campanulaceae, eventually magnified itself into 91 species, producing 9 percent of the total species in pre-human Hawai'i. Now that's a real pioneer success story!

Another curious fact: although Hawai'i is closest to North America, most of its native plants suggest origins in Asia. The American contribution might be as small as 18 percent.

This book shows very few of these true native plants—not because they are uninteresting but because they lie outside the awareness of most people, whether tourists or residents. Most survive far off the beaten path. Today, about 50 percent of the Hawaiian landscape consists of cattle pastures and 30 percent of plantations and towns, with just 20 percent truly wild. Even in those wild areas, the natives are having trouble competing with aggressive plants that have naturalized—that is, escaped from cultivation. About 38 percent of Hawai'i's native plants are thought to be extinct or are living on the brink of extinction.

What happened to the natives? Of course the answer is this: human beings arrived, eventually, bringing their landscape-disturbing practices and their favored animals and plants.

The earliest evidence of Polynesian arrival points to some time in the fourth or fifth century A.D. In their canoes these first settlers carried the plants that they used for food, shelter, and clothing. All but two of the plant species they brought have naturalized into the landscape, and these plants seem to most people quintessentially "Hawaiian plants." These "canoe plants" (as some call them) include taro, sugar cane, banana, coconut, sweet potato, and a kind of mulberry Hawaiians call wauke, from which they once fashioned their pounded-bark cloth called kapa. The Hawaiians were exceptional gardeners and stone-builders, and the first observers from the Western world remarked on the fertility of the agriculture and the size and vigor of the island population.

So the Polynesians changed the look of the landscape. But they did not introduce a high number of new plant species. The botanical explosion had to wait until Cook's arrival in 1778.

During the past 200-plus years, the look of floral Hawai'i has changed phenomenally. Because the islands have tall mountains and many microclimates, you can grow just about anything in Hawai'i (anything that doesn't require a hard winter freeze). And so people have done. The fences of Hawaiian gardens are very porous—by that I mean plants escape into the wild quite easily. Hawai'i has become a showplace for the flowering glory of the Earth's tropical and temperate regions.

However people may feel about the plight of the native plants, they can't help being delighted by the beauty of Hawai'i's ever-changing garden-scape. In fact, botanizing—that is, enjoying plants in their variations of flower and leaf—is reason enough to make a trip to the islands.

## THE OFFICIAL ISLAND FLOWERS

A Hawai'i tradition dating back to the 1920s gives each island its own official flower. (I say "flower" despite the fact that several are foliage plants and one is not a plant at all—the small sea shells of Ni'ihau.) At parades, Lei Day festivities on May 1, and other public occasions, you will see the islands represented by lei of these flowers, each associated with a specific color.

The Hawai'i state flower is a native yellow hibiscus, *Hibiscus brackenridgei*. The Hawaiian language common name is pua aloalo or ma'o hau hele.

LEFT: The kukui tree, which is also the state tree, stands for Moloka'i. *Aleurites moluccana* is a Polynesian introduction, a member of family Euphorbiaceae.

BOTTOM LEFT: O'ahu claims the golden native flower called 'ilima, botanical name *Sida fallax*, a relative of the hibiscus.

BOTTOM RIGHT: Maui is figured as the pink rose called loke lani.

OPPOSITE PAGE: Representing the island of Hawai'i is the lehua blossom, from the native tree *Metrosideros polymorpha*. The Hawaiian name is 'ōhi'a lehua.

Ann Cecil

Mokihana, a native member of the citrus family, represents Kaua'i. The botanical name is *Pelea anisata*.

IHP Archive

Veronica Carmona

ABOVE: Lāna'i is symbolized by a gray, thready lei plant called kauna'oa. This plant, *Cuscuta sandwichiana*, has given up its leaves and learned to parasitize other plants.

LEFT: The pūpū, or small shells made into famous Ni'ihau shell lei, represent that small island.

The symbol for the island Kaho'olawe, which is unpopulated but equal to the other islands in its spiritual significance, is hinahina—a silver, thready, hard-to-find native plant. Nowadays people use this substitute, *Tillandsia usneoides* or Spanish moss (see the bromeliads on page 60).

## Garden plants that got away and settled down to live in Hawai'i:

| | |
|---|---|
| air plant | lamb's quarters |
| alfalfa | lettuce |
| alyssum | lobelia |
| basil | marigold |
| begonia | nasturtium |
| blackberry | nettle |
| buttercup | pennyroyal |
| California poppy | potato |
| carrot | radish |
| castor bean | ragweed |
| chili pepper | sage |
| clover | Scotch broom |
| cocklebur | sisal |
| coriander | snapdragon |
| cotton | Spanish broom |
| crabgrass | spearmint |
| dandelion | spider plant |
| fennel | strawberry |
| flax | sunflower |
| forget-me-not | thistle |
| goldenrod | tobacco |
| gorse | tomato |
| heliotrope | yarrow |
| honeysuckle | zinnia |
| horehound | |

This list does not include trees, and the tree list is a very interesting list, too, ranging from mesquite to avocado.

# Wild Ones

These plants came to Hawai'i—on their own or by Polynesian canoe—well before Captain Cook.

# *Agavaceae*  Cordyline fruticosa  •  **ti, ki**

Of all the plants that the early Hawaiians put to use, the ti (pronounced "tee") is certainly the most versatile. Its flat, oval leaves—as clean and pliable as stiff paper—made an excellent light construction material for roof-thatching, raingear, sandals, rope, and clothing (the so-called "grass skirt"—a hula look that was adopted in more modern times). Ti leaves also make an all-purpose kitchen aid, serving as food wrappers, plates, oven liners, and cups. Musicians fashioned whistles from the leaves; children went grass-sliding on them. This usefulness was enhanced by the fact that ti is so easy to grow—just stick a chunk of stem in the ground. The meat of the root, baked, provided a sweet sticky food from which the Hawaiians fermented a mild alcoholic beverage. Shortly after Cook's arrival, they learned the skill of distilling that brew into a kind of brandy called 'ōkolehao—an indulgence that contributed to the weakening of the race.

*Cordyline fruticosa* is part of the agave family, related to yucca, sisal, and the century plant. Originally from southeast Asia, it was planted throughout the Pacific by the colonizing Polynesians. Its growth habit is simple—a stiff vertical stem crowned with a tight spiral of fresh leaves. Varieties come in all shades of red, but the green grandaddy is the one still considered to be an essential Hawaiian dooryard plant—both as an emblem of good luck and as a ready supply of table ornamentation.

# *Apocynaceae*    Alyxia oliviformis  •  **maile**

Back then and right now, the people of Hawai'i felt and feel a special love for the fragrant bark and leaves of this wild forest climber. Pulled into long streamers and twined together, strips of maile make a scarf-like lei that is traditionally worn by any person experiencing a grand moment. This plant embodies Laka, the goddess of the hula.

Maile (pronounced "my lay") is partly vine, partly shrub. Because it assumes a variety of forms and leaf-shapes, the old Hawaiians gave it several names, and modern botanists have tried far more. Current wisdom, though, gives maile one name as a species—*Alyxia oliviformis* (the leaf is somewhat olive-leaf-like in form)—and admits that the plant comes in many shapes. The genus *Alyxia* includes about 120 species that occur throughout the Pacific rim, but maile itself is endemic to Hawai'i. Regardless of its leaf shape, its spicy vanilla fragrance (which intensifies as the leaves wilt) conveys the same honor.

The botanical family that includes maile has a knack for showy flowers, so it is represented in this book by several blossoms in the following chapters: oleander, yellow oleander, allamanda, periwinkle, and mandevilla. The same family also includes one of Hawai'i's most familiar trees, the plumeria.

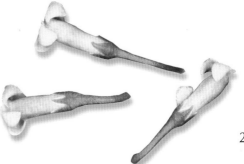

21

# *Araceae*  Alocasia macrorrhiza · **elephant's ear, 'ape**

Don't say "'ape," as though this is a monkey. "Awe pay" is right. In fact, "awe pay" feels like the right thing to say when you encounter a fleshy leaf more than three feet long on a waist-high stem. To grow leaves this big, 'ape needs its favored habitat—a deep, moist gulch where the wind hardly stirs. Polynesians brought 'ape, a native of India and Sri Lanka, wherever they traveled. This plant's log-like, ground-hugging stem, whenever baked, ensured survival when better-tasting foods ran short.

The philodendron family, with its arrowhead-shaped leaves, its spike-in-a-cup flowers, and its water-loving habit, has been wildly successful in the tropics—107 genera and about three thousand species. It includes anthurium, calla, spathiphyllum, caladium, monstera, philodendron, dieffenbachia, and (most important of all for Hawai'i) taro.

# *Araceae*  Colocasia esculenta • **taro, kalo**

Taro is the mother plant of Hawaiian culture—not just the "daily bread" of nourishment but also the abiding symbol of social harmony. The plant is cultivated throughout the Pacific and southeast Asia, but nowhere with the industry and ingenuity of the ancient Hawaiians.

Taro is a marsh plant, so the Hawaiians excelled in the construction of waterworks and clever flowing ponds (called lo'i) in which the farmers waded. They developed three hundred varieties of taro, some adapted to dryland conditions. Their folklore describes taro as the older sibling of the human race, and people saw the growth habit of taro—in expanding clusters of offshoots called ʻohā—as a perfect metaphor for a well-run family, or ʻohana.

All parts of the plant are eaten, from the starchy corm (root) to the spinach-like leaves. Uncooked, the plant is acrid because its flesh is full of sharp crystals of calcium oxalate. Cooking eliminates their bite. Once cooked, the corm is generally pounded to make poi, an excellent carbohydrate food. The cooked greens, called lūʻau, are a nutritious source of minerals and vitamins A, B, and C.

# *Asteraceae* Argyroxiphium sandwicense • **silversword, 'āhinahina**

Eons ago a daisy-like plant from North America found its way to the Hawaiian islands and evolved into this botanical marvel. Growing in the extreme high-altitude volcanic cinder deserts of Maui's Haleakalā and Hawai'i island's Mauna Kea, the silversword forms a moon-like sphere with its numerous scimitar-shaped succulent leaves. The plant's heat-reflective fur of white hairs keeps the leaves from parching to death. At life's end the plant performs its one act of blooming—at the average age of twelve and some time between June and November—by shooting up a flower spike that can be six feet tall and contain six hundred resinous purple flowers. Then, having set seed, the plant shrivels and blows apart in the alpine winds.

Silverswords formerly blanketed many acres of Haleakalā Crater. But by the early twentieth century the attacks of newly arrived insects, goats, and human collectors had shaved the population down to fewer than a hundred plants. Thanks to national park controls, this species is recovering but still endangered.

"Argyroxiphium" might look impossible to pronounce, but the job gets easier when you split the word into its two Greek roots. "Argyro" means silver. "Xiphium" means sword (pronounce the "x" as a "z.") Actually there are five species of this Hawai'i-only genus. The others are rare, remote bog plants, one of which is now probably extinct.

# Convolvulaceae

Ipomoea spp • **morning glory, koali**

Ipomoea pes-caprae • **beach morning glory, pōhuehue**

Ipomoea batatas • **sweet potato, 'uala**

The largest genus of the morning-glory family, *Ipomoea* includes five hundred species spread throughout the tropics of the world. In Hawai'i fourteen species are native or naturalized, and five more can be found testing the fences of people's gardens. Prior to 1871, Chinese immigrants brought the edible morning glory *Ipomoea aquatica*, known to Asian cooking as the ung-choi, and it has naturalized around Hawaiian streams and ponds.

ABOVE: *Ipomoea spp*, morning glory

LEFT: *Ipomoea pes-caprae*, beach morning glory

RIGHT: *Ipomoea batatas*, sweet potato

# *Epacridaceae*  Styphelia tameiameiae • **pūkiawe**

An indigenous plant that also occurs in the Marquesas Islands, pūkiawe is familiar to hikers in the national parks. It's a tough, stiff, small-leaved shrub whose small red or pink berries brighten the trailside. Quite variable in form, these plants occur naturally from two thousand feet elevation to the mountain summits, thriving on arid lava as well as forest and bog. Hawaiians added pūkiawe to their lei for the extra color. If a kapu chief wanted to dispense with the rules that separated him from common people, he would use the incense of burning pūkiawe as a spiritual fumigation. The wood was used to cremate the bodies of outlaws.

# *Ericaceae*    Vaccinium reticulatum  •  **'ōhelo**

Hawai'i has three endemic species of what could be termed the Hawaiian blueberry (or huckleberry, or cranberry—these plants are all in the same genus), although islanders go by the Hawaiian name 'ōhelo. People know them for the same reason they know the related plants—tasty fruit, which is often made into jam, syrup, or the equivalent of cranberry sauce. The little shrubs (one to two feet high) are common around Kīlauea volcano. The Hawaiians felt that 'ōhelo, with its red berries, was sacred to the fire goddess Pele. They would offer a branch to Pele—tossing it into the seething caldera—before eating the fruit themselves. This custom triggered one of the most dramatic moments of early Hawaiian history. In 1824, four years after the arrival of Western missionaries, the high chiefess Kapi'olani hiked down into the caldera, threw rocks, ate 'ōhelo berries, and announced: "Jehovah is my god. All the gods of Hawai'i are vain." The fact that she survived greatly facilitated the work of the missionaries.

# Goodeniaceae

Scaevola sericea • **beach naupaka, naupaka kahakai**

One of Hawai'i's most common seaside plants, this shrub grows throughout tropical and subtropical Pacific and Indian Ocean coasts. The flower is pale yellow-green, fading to white and streaked with purple. Berries are white. As the flowers form, they split along one seam and fan out, making what looks like half a flower.

Hawai'i also has species of *Scaevola* that are endemic to the islands and collectively termed "mountain naupaka." The fact that there are similar half-flowers along the shoreline and on the mountainside led to the invention of a couple of romantic folk tales. In one, two lovers are separated by the jealous rage of the goddess Pele. The man became the mountain naupaka; the woman became its beach counterpart. To bring together the two half-flowers is to reunite the ill-fated pair.

# *Malvaceae*

Hibiscus, various • **hibiscus, aloalo**

In Hawai'i the genus *Hibiscus* is represented by five endemic species, two that
occur naturally in other regions, three
that have escaped from gardens, and
many more cultivated showpieces than
are easy to count. For cultivated types,
see pages 96, 97 and 98.

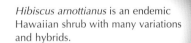

*Hibiscus arnottianus* is an endemic
Hawaiian shrub with many variations
and hybrids.

## Sida fallax • 'ilima

This indigenous relative of the hibiscus grows as a small or even prostrate shrub with comparatively small, velvety leaves. The allure of 'ilima ("ee-lee-ma," with the accent equal on all syllables) derives from its simple, rather flat, nickel-size flowers that shine in hues of gold. This is the principal lei flower of pre-discovery Hawai'i. Today an 'ilima lei conveys honor by associating the wearer with ancient tradition. It also represents a lot of tedious finger-work, as the paper-thin flowers are strung face-to-face. It is said to be one form of Laka, the goddess of the hula. 'Ilima is one of the few native plants that has achieved growing popularity as a landscaping plant.

34

# *Musaceae*   Musa x paradisiaca • **banana, maiʻa**

You might think that the banana is a small tree, but what you see is really a tightly clasped stalk of leaves—rather like a gigantic celery. The heart of the banana is underground. The stalk is so tightly clasped that new leaves, pushing up the center from below, have to coat themselves with something like talcum powder to break the friction. The stalk finishes with an enormous flower stem that hangs from above, fanning out into the familiar "hands." Then the whole stalk falls, to be replaced by several side-shoots or keiki (children).

Being one of the great food plants of tropical Asia and the Pacific, the banana has been anciently cultivated into hundreds of varieties and hybrids. The early Hawaiians brought it to the islands and developed an estimated seventy varieties, twenty of which remain. They saw an analogy between banana trunks and men. (One old saying: "A man is like a banana the day it bears fruit"—in other words, when his work is done, he dies.) And the Hawaiians took such symbols quite seriously. This was a men-only food. Women who ate bananas were executed. Banana stalks were used for lining the imu, or underground ovens, and for rolling canoes across land.

Banana fibers provided lei-making thread, the sap made a dye, and the nectar was fed to babies.

The banana family includes ornamental flowers pictured elsewhere in this book—heliconias, the bird of paradise, and the travelers palm.

IHP Archive

# *Piperaceae*

**Piper methysticum • 'awa, kava**

A strong narcotic herb, 'awa can be recognized by its large heart-shaped leaves, its narrow flower spikes, and its twiggy stems with swollen joints. A close relative of pepper, 'awa originated in the islands of or near Indonesia and was carried by aboriginal explorers throughout the Pacific. The Hawaiians knew more than fifteen varieties, out of which they made a ceremonial beverage. The recipe: chew the roots and spit them into a bowl, add water, stir, and strain. The first effect of the drink is a refreshing stimulation. Continued indulgence leads to hypnotic numbness, weak vision, and a scaly skin condition. The leaves of 'awa's close relative *Piper betle* provide a similar stimulation to the betel-nut chewers of tropical Asia.

# *Sapindaceae*   Dodonea viscosa • ʻaʻaliʻi

A resourceful shrub that grows as tall as thirty feet, ʻaʻaliʻi (ah-ah-lee-ee) is not only a sturdy citizen of Hawaiʻi's dryland forest but also a naturally occurring resident of most of the warm parts of the planet. Labeled by its botanical name, dodonea, this plant is also well represented in the commercial nursery trade. A rather nondescript shrub with oblong leaves, ʻaʻaliʻi is recognized primarily for its seed capsules—papery, winged, clustered at the branch tips, and often bright red or red-purple. These colorful clusters, picked and strung together, make a very traditional and long-lasting lei. The Hawaiians of old had many uses for the hard, brown-red wood of the ʻaʻaliʻi, excellent timber for house construction or for spears. The fruit capsules, when boiled, produce an excellent red

dye. The plants represents endurance. The old boast: "I am a wind-resisting ʻaʻaliʻi." In other words, you can't knock me down.

# *Zingiberaceae*  Curcuma longa · **turmeric, 'ōlena**

For centuries the juicy root of turmeric has been used as a spice and a dye for food, especially in its homeland India. Powdered turmeric is the key ingredient in curry powder. The Polynesians brought the plant to Hawai'i, calling it 'ōlena (oh-lay-na). The Hawaiians used 'ōlena ceremonially to purify places and people. The steamed root was eaten as medicine and used to produce a deep orange dye for kapa cloth. The raw juice of the root cured earaches and provided a light yellow dye. The stemless leaves arise in spring and die back in the fall. The short flower stalks come right out of the ground and show colors ranging from yellow to pink.

# *Zingiberaceae*   Zingiber zerumbet • **shampoo ginger, 'awapuhi**

In the lower parts of damp forests, the shampoo ginger or 'awapuhi is a common sight, often forming a continuous shin-high ground cover. Hawaiians brought this plant to the islands and used its large aromatic underground stems to perfume their kapa cloth. The mature flower head is naturally saturated with a fragrant, slimy juice that the Hawaiians used for shampoo and to quench their thirst. They used the leaves to flavor meat. Ashes of the leaves had medicinal value.

These two Polynesian-introduced zingibers—'ōlena and 'awapuhi—are closely related to the commercial ginger root and to several sweet-smelling roadside plants that are pictured in the next section of this book.

Donna Allison

# Roadside Plants

Some species of flowering plants escaped from Hawaiian gardens so early and so successfully that they now behave more like natives than like cultivars. Here are some plants that are likely to catch your eye as you travel in remote places.

# *Cactaceae*  Opuntia ficus-indica • **prickly pear , pānini**

Visitors to Hawaiʻi, expecting lush tropical jungle, are often surprised to find themselves driving past these tree-sized plates of spine. Pānini is Hawaiʻi's most commonly encountered escaped cactus. The Hawaiian name means "very unfriendly wall." Unfriendliness, however, was not Don Francisco Paul de Marin's motivation for bringing these plants from Veracruz, Mexico, some time prior to 1809. As the name "prickly pear" suggests, the panini bears fruit, either red or greenish-yellow. The barrel-shaped fruit (technically a berry) forms along the edge of the plates, looking like stubby fingers on a wide hand. Carefully harvested (tongs help) and stripped of their spiny skin, these cactus berries reward caution with a juicy sweetness.

# *Heliconiaceae*

Heliconia, various • **heliconia**

At least twenty-two species of these extravagant jungle bloomers have come from their home in South America to gardens in Hawai'i. So far, three species have escaped cultivation, and others are no doubt testing the boundaries. As with their close relatives the bananas, helico-nias send up sturdy, herbaceous leaf stalks from an underground foundation. In some species the stalks tower to twenty feet. The blooms arise on their own leafless stalks, typically hidden in the plant's thicket of foliage. The actual flowers are rather small, but they sit snugly inside enormous, bright-colored bracts shaped like narrow boats. The bracts typically rise, or hang, in a flat plane, alternating in a stair-step fashion.

43

# Melastomataceae

Tibouchina urvilleana  •  **glory bush**

Hawai'i botanist Otto Degener wrote, "For the privilege of growing this beautiful plant in the garden, the flower-lover should conscientiously keep it from escaping into the open." This native of Brazil likes to form impenetrable thickets (head-high or worse) that swallow the endemic landscape. And yet it's showy enough to be a car-stopper—large red-purple flowers, red flower buds, and deeply veined, hairy leaves with a silvery underside. This aggressive beauty was introduced on Hawai'i island in 1910 and has spread all the way to Kaua'i, where it has severely altered natural areas such as Kilohana Crater.

# *Onagraceae*   Oenothera spp • **evening primrose**

Paul Wood

The evening primrose, in the form of one species or another, has managed to colonize all the continents except Antarctica. Three types have taken root in mountain areas of the Hawaiian islands. The "evening" in the name refers to the fact that flowers bloom each day near sunset. As the next day passes, they redden and fall. The family Onagraceae, which includes the fuchsias, is unusual in the world of botany because its flowers are designed by the number four, rather than five or three. The name "oenothera" suggests that the ancient Greeks used one member of this genus to flavor "oeno"—that is, wine.

# *Orchidaceae*   Spathoglottis plicata  •  **various wild orchids**

Three types of orchid are endemic to Hawai'i, and four have escaped from gardens. The most commonly seen is the Philippine (or Malayan) ground orchid, *Spathoglottis plicata*, which grows almost four feet tall in grassy fields. You find it at lower elevations on all the major islands. Leaves are broad and pleated. Flowers range in color from dark purple to pale pink. An Asian native called the bamboo orchid, *Arundina graminifolia*, has narrow leaves, lavender but yellow-throated flowers, and cane-like stems. Since 1945 it has started appearing in disturbed soils on all major islands.

46

# *Papaveraceae*

Argemone glauca · **prickly poppy, pua kala**

The poppies, close relatives of evening primrose, are known for their bright flowers and, of course, for the fact that the milky sap of some species possesses a narcotic quality that has given both relief and grief to the human race. In fact, the ancient Hawaiians eased their toothaches and ulcers with the one species of poppy that is endemic to the Islands—*Argemone glauca*. Plants in the genus *Argemone* are also known as prickly poppies, a reference to their spiny stems and leaves. The pua kala has a six-petaled white flower about three inches across, with a poppy's characteristic bristle of yellow stamens clustered around a red-tipped pistil. It's also common to see a yellow-flowered species, *Argemone mexicana*, which is native to the West Indies and Mexico. Three other kinds of poppies have escaped within limited ranges, including the California state flower, *Eschscholtzia californica*.

*Argemone glauca*, prickly poppy

*Argemone mexicana*

# *Poaceae*   Coix lachryma-jobi • **Job's tears, pū'ohe'ohe**

People like to harvest the seeds of Job's tears and string them into all manner of things, including lei, rosaries, purses, and table mats. In India the seeds are ground for cereal. In fact, Job's tears is a close relative of corn, and it has something of that corn habit—the stalk, and the hefty leaves that clasp around it. But this world-traveling cousin of corn is much more dainty. Technically Job's tears is a weed, but it's certainly not a pest. Rather, it appears as a welcome surprise on streamside hikes in windward valleys. The seeds turn from green to black, then shade gradually to white.

# *Verbenaceae*   Lantana camara • **lantana**

Because lantana blooms continuously and so brightly, gardeners in some parts of the world cultivate it. But in Hawai'i people regard lantana with a sigh and a shake of the head. Armed with aggressive thorns and inclined to form dense thickets, this malodorous shrub has become a serious pest of rangeland, agricultural regions, and forests—so serious, in fact, that biologists have identified and introduced numerous insect species that parasitize this plant. These attempts at bio-control have not proven very successful. Lantana is common along roadsides on all the main islands. And its flowers, which come in all the colors of an Easter basket, are pretty to see.

# *Zingiberaceae* Gingers, various

*(See also pages 38 and 39 for two types of ginger known in pre-discovery Hawai'i.)*

At least nine species of ginger have slipped away from the supervision of gardeners and found their places in the Hawaiian landscape, most commonly in wet areas—windward roadsides, stream banks, and jungle verges. In summer and fall, bloom time, you see people parked by the road cutting and cleaning the sturdy flower stalks. The flowers are delicate. But, preserved in a hefty vase, they fill the house with a subtle, sensual fragrance. The ginger family is known for its thick underground stems and cool aromatic vegetative parts that yield spices (cardamon, ginger root, turmeric), dye, perfume, medicine, fiber, and (in Hawai'i) lei. The family evolved in south and southeast Asia. Many varieties were brought to Hawai'i by early immigrants from China.

*Alpinia speciosa*, shell ginger, 'awapuhi luheluhe

Paul Wood

*Hedychium coronarium*, white ginger, 'awapuhi ke'oke'o

*Hedychium flavescens*, yellow ginger, 'awapuhi melemele

*Phaeomeria magnifica*, torch ginger, 'awapuhi ko'oko'o

50

*Hedychium gardnerianum,*
kāhili ginger, ʻawapuhi kāhili

# Garden Soft-Stemmed Plants

This section looks at Hawai'i's garden plants that are generally low in stature, with fleshy stems that sprawl or rise to just a few feet high.

# Amaryllidaceae

The amaryllis family is so closely related to the lilies that many botanists bundle them together under the name Liliaceae. Although poorly represented in the native flora—only three endemic species and one indigenous—this group contributes many prized flowers to the repertoire of home gardeners.

**Crinum augustum 'Queen Emma' • Queen Emma lily**

The Queen Emma lily holds a place of honor in Hawaiian horticulture because of its association with island royalty. Queen Emma, the widely admired wife of Kamehameha IV, promoted health care for her people by establishing the Queen's Hospital. During the late 1800s she developed beautiful gardens on her Kaua'i estate—now the site of Allerton Garden—and this plant was one of her favorites. A native of Mauritius and the Seychelles, *Crinum augustum* grows from a six-inch bulb and sends up bouquets of long, lax flowers on flattened stems about two feet high. These plants like moist conditions under the protective canopy of trees.

*Hippeastrum puniceum,* amaryllis, Barbados lily

## Hippeastrum puniceum • **amaryllis, Barbados lily**

The well-known amaryllis flower, which originated in the American tropics, has long been a favorite of bulb gardeners. Many of the seventy-plus species of *Hippeastrum* have been hybridized into countless variations. In Hawai'i you find them popping up along irrigation ditches and in moist pastures.

One type of amaryllis commonly found in the older gardens of Hawai'i is the bright and shining "Pink Lady."

"Pink Lady"

**Polianthes tuberosa** • **tuberose**

A bewitching fragrance gives this fleshy flower a large fan club. A native of Mexico, tuberose grows in moist soil from tuberous underground stems, shooting up flowering spikes clad with grass-like leaves. Flowers are lightly pink-tinged in bud, pure cream white in maturity. Tuberose is commonly grown in Hawai'i, to be strung into lei or sold as cut flowers.

# *Araceae*   Anthurium, various • **anthurium**

The leading figures of Hawai'i's cut-flower trade, anthuriums are the focus of many an island gardener's passion. Given the right conditions—humidity and protection from sun and wind—they thrive in Hawai'i's climate. Also, they offer tremendous variety—some five hundred species evolved in the American tropics. And of course their inimitable "flowers" possess a great charm. The true flowers of the anthurium are minute, and they arrange themselves on a curving spike known as a spadix. This spike juts from a highly specialized leaf—heart-shaped, glossy, and capable of infinite color variations—known as a spathe. The spathe is so waxy and shiny that people often take it to be artificial. The inflorescence will last for months on the plant, and for weeks in a vase. Anthuriums grow via underground stems, throwing out relatively few, large leaves.

# Asteraceae

Wedelia trilobata • **wedelia**

A standard groundcover, especially at the condos, resorts, and shopping centers, wedelia responds to almost any abuse with cheerful vitality. Shiny green leaves in pairs cover the stringy stems that run along the ground rooting, one over the other, forming a thick mat. Leaves are fleshy with a toothed tip, usually three-lobed (sometimes oval). Flowers are yellow daisies in miniature, about half an inch across. Fortunately for island ecology, this plant rarely produces any seeds in Hawai'i. In its desire to spread, though, wedelia has escaped from gardens throughout the state.

# Balsaminaceae

Impatiens wallerana • **impatiens**

An irrepressible, cheerful flower of shady garden areas, impatiens grows up to two feet tall on succulent stems. The plants bloom continuously in colors that range from deep red through purple, orange, pink, to true white. Flowers are an inch and a half across and bear a thin, curving spur below. When the fleshy green fruit is ripe, it snaps open, throwing seeds about. This impulsive habit led to its scientific name and to one of its common names, "touch me not." Common in cultivation, this African native escapes freely into the verges of Hawai'i's rainforests.

# *Bromeliaceae*  Bromeliads, various

The 1,400-plus members of the pineapple family are all natives of tropical and subtropical America. Leaves are generally long, stiff, and spiny, and they typically form a basal cup that collects and holds water. Most bromeliads are epiphytes— that is, they grow above the ground by fixing their flimsy roots onto rocks or larger plants. The great attraction of bromeliads, and what makes them a fixation of plant hobbyists, is the apparent miracle of their blooming. Out of scrawny rosettes of tired-looking foliage emerge flower stalks of truly fantastic form and color.

This group also includes Spanish moss, *Tillandsia usneoides* (see page 17), famous for its habit of draping live oak trees in the southernmost United States with long silvery beards. In Hawai'i, Spanish moss is made into lei, so you'll often see it hanging from baskets suspended around the house. The island name for this plant is "hinahina"—in the old days people called it "Mr. Dole," a reference to the long beard of Hawai'i's first territorial governor.

# *Cannaceae*   Canna indica • **canna, aliʻipoe**

The ginger-like canna family has but one genus, which is native to tropical America. This one species has been carried worldwide and cultivated in many forms, with flowers in various combinations of yellow and red, leaves ranging from green to purple. Botanically speaking, the flowers are odd because the colored structures that seem to be petals are actually sterile stamens—the true petals are narrow and inconspicuous. The seed case has a warty shell and splits open along three lines. The round, hard, black seeds have evoked the name "Indian shot." Canna came to Hawaiʻi shortly after Captain Cook arrived. The Hawaiians soon started stringing the seeds into lei and using them as rattle-beads in hula performances. The plant found its wild place in the wet forests of all the main islands.

# *Commelinaceae*

**Dichorisandra thyrsiflora • blue ginger**

What folks in Hawai'i call "blue ginger" is actually a close relative of such indoor potted plants as the wandering jew and the spiderwort, as well as the popular groundcover *Rhoeo*, commonly called Moses-in-a-cradle. This plant grows on stems three to six feet tall with shiny leaves arranged in spiral formation. It requires shade, water, and plenty of fertilizer. But it rewards the effort with terminal flower spikes that glow with an unusual purple-blue color.

# *Iridaceae*    Crocosmia x crocosmiflora • **montbretia**

The rich orange flowers of montbretia, alternating on zigzag stems, can be found brightening the sides of upcountry roads and trails on all major islands of Hawai'i. In fact, it does the same all over the tropical Americas—poke out of the thickets with its narrow, grassy knee-high leaves. Hardy as it is, this member of the iris family is not a native of anywhere. It's a gardeners' hybrid of two plants from South Africa. Incapable of producing fertile seeds, it spreads itself via fat underground stems called corms. (People sometimes call this plant by its old botanical name, tritonia.)

Donna Allison

# *Lamiaceae*

## Plectranthus scutellarioides • **coleus**

Foliage upstages flower in this widely cultivated perennial herb. The leaves come in seemingly endless variegations of red, purple, yellow, and green. Originally from east Asia, coleus has spread throughout the tropics, carried around by gardeners purely for the pleasure of seeing its colorful leaves. In Hawai'i coleus has found a home in forests on all the major islands. Its square stems and its spikes of small blue, irregularly shaped flowers show that this plant is clearly a member of the mint family (even though it has no mint-like fragrance). Wise gardeners are quick to snap off the flower spikes, thereby forcing these plants to stay with the sole purpose for which they are grown—pumping out bushy mats of shameless leaves.

# *Marantaceae*  Calathea zebrina · **zebra plant**

The zebra plant, a type of *Calathea* from Brazil, attracts home gardeners with its showy leaves. These leaves unfold in a spiral pattern, rising just a foot or two above the ground on short, unbranched stems. The blades are narrow ovals up to two feet long, striped with slanting lines of yellow-green and dark olive green. The undersides are red-purple.

Dendrobium

Epidendrum

# *Orchidaceae*

**Dendrobium, Cattleya, Vanda, Oncidium, Vanilla fragrans, Phalaenopsis, Cymbidium, Epidendrum**

The orchid family includes more than six hundred genera—or perhaps a thousand genera. It comprises some twenty thousand species—or some say over thirty thousand species. The point is that Orchidaceae is a huge group, and its study is endless. The hobby—or is it mania?—of orchid cultivation has long been popular. Hawai'i has a large and well-established orchid industry, with a strong emphasis on the genus *Dendrobium*. Various societies and networks of breeders, both professional and amateur, have made Hawai'i one of the world's great centers for study of this amazing group.

Orchids in the genus *Epidendrum* are a common sight in Hawai'i's backyards. Requiring little care, they deliver masses of small flowers.

Vanda

Brassia

Dendrobium

Dendrobium

68

Cattleya

# *Strelitziaceae*  Strelitzia reginae · **bird of paradise**

Close relative of the heliconia and the banana, the bird of paradise is widely cultivated in temperate climates but does exceptionally well in Hawai'i. Plants form stemless clumps of leaves three or four feet tall. Flowers arise on stalks as tall as the leaves. The "birds," of course, are the flowers themselves, which flare out from the sturdy "beak" to flash their orange feathers and blue tongues. Given water and time, these plants are easy to grow. The primary maintenance involves a frequent cutting-away of dead stalks and sorry-looking foliage. The bird of paradise is prized in the cut-flower trade for use in arrangement of long-stem "tropicals."

**Strelitzia nicolai** • **giant bird of paradise**

This tree-like species of bird of paradise can grow as high as twenty feet. Flowers look very much like the common bird, but bigger and not so brightly colored— blue and white only. Plants will branch at the base, producing over time a dozen or more thick trunks.

## Ravenala madagascariensis

- **travelers palm**

Although its height (as much as thirty feet tall) and its stout trunk would suggest that this plant belongs in a book about trees, the travelers palm needs to be mentioned here because of its kinship to the bird of paradise. It, too, bears feather-like flowers that flare up from a beak-like case. As with its cousin the banana, travelers palm bears huge, sail-like leaves that tatter into ribbons as they are shaken by strong winds. Unlike nearly all plants, this one chooses to grow with a curious flatness— the leaves all emerge on the same plane, spreading out like an enormous fan. Rainwater gets concentrated at the hollow base of each leaf. Hence the common name—parched travelers can find reservoirs of liquid refreshment here.

# Garden Shrubs

Plants with woody
stems make up the larger
architecture of the garden.
They mask foundations,
form hedges, screen views,
or sometimes (if pruned)
provide canopy for shade-
loving plants below.

# Acanthaceae

The acanthus family with its two thousand five hundred species is widespread in tropical regions and provides Hawaiian gardens with many shrubs favored for their handsome foliage and colorful flowers. One member with commercial value, the Mexican indigo, has naturalized itself on Moloka'i. The genus *Thunbergia* appears in our vines chapter.

## Justicia brandegeana
### • shrimp plant

The shrimp plant is a weak-stemmed, rather slight shrub prized for its curious blossoms. The flowers form a curving spike up to four inches long encased in overlapping bracts that are brick-red. A native of Mexico, the shrimp plant can get up to eight feet tall, particularly if it has a fence or other structure to lean on.

## Justicia carnea • **Brazilian plume flower**

*Justicia* is a large genus, having some three hundred species located in tropical regions throughout the world. One species with a modest white flower (*Justicia betonica*) likes the Hawaiian climate so much that it tends to become a serious weed pest. This is not the case, however, with Brazilian plume flower, which prefers greenhouse-type conditions—rich soil and protection from direct sunlight. This spindly shrub gets up to six feet tall. The brilliant flowers form large clusters in the pink-to-red color range.

## Pseuderanthemum reticulatum • **eldorado**

The eldorado comes to Hawai'i from southern Polynesia. It is commonly used as a low hedge plant in sea-level communities. The common name refers to its lush golden leaves, which contrast vividly with the older dark green foliage. The loose flower spikes have a rose-purple hue.

## Sanchezia nobilis • **sanchezia**

A shrub with origins in Ecuador, the sanchezia can get up to six feet tall. It has two attractions. First, its leaves are large—up to eighteen inches long. In the variety called '*glaucophylla,*' dark green contrasts sharply with pale yellow leaf veins. Then when sanchezia blooms it throws out terminal spikes two inches long enclosed in bracts that are vividly red. This plant can be aggressive and weedy in the home garden.

Gerald Carr

# *Apocynaceae*   Cascabela thevetia • **yellow oleander, be-still tree**

This cousin of the more common oleander has something of the same growth habit—it's a sturdy, vertical shrub that can push up to the size of a small tree. Foliage is so shiny that it seems to shimmer in the breeze, hence one of its common names, the be-still tree. Plants bloom continuously with funnel-shaped yellow flowers, mildly fragrant, clustered at the branch tips. This species contains a strong heart depressant, called thevetin, so all parts of this plant are poisonous to people and livestock.

## Nerium oleander • **oleander**

The oleander's native habitat ranges from Iran to Japan. It is such a sturdy, reliable shrub, resistant to drought, salt, and raging winds, that it has become a landscaping standard in all temperate regions, including Hawai'i. No matter where it grows—along freeways, under the canopy of trees—oleander blooms non-stop. Flowers are single or double, usually sweetly scented, and colored red, pink, rose, salmon, or white. Plants can get up to twenty feet tall. Every part of the oleander is highly poisonous. Keep the dry sticks out of your barbecue.

# *Asclepiadaceae*   Calotropis gigantea • **crown flower**

The crown flower, or giant Indian milk-weed, produces the floral ingredients for a lei of royal symbolism. The petals of this thick, sweet-smelling blossom roll back to expose a peculiar curling structure that looks something like a miniature crown carved out of ivory. Hawaiʻi's last queen, Liliʻuokalani, loved these little emblems. Today, lei-makers string crown flowers, with or without the petals, in honor of the queen and of the (fallen) Hawaiian monarchy. This shrub has thick, downy stems and leaves. It favors coastal areas, where it can grow to fifteen feet tall. Typical of milkweeds, it produces a latex

or milky sap that can irritate the skin. Medicinal in small amounts, this latex is poisonous in quantity. For this reason, the crown flower is host to caterpillars of the monarch butterfly, which gain an immunity from predators by assimilating the toxic juice. In its native India, the crown flower is sacred to Siva, and its buds are figured on the passion-darts shot by Kama, god of love. You find two color variations in Hawaiʻi, white and pale lavender. Also, a form with a delicate, miniature flower of purple and white is gaining popularity.

# *Bignoniaceae*   Tecoma stans • **yellow elder**

The bignonia family has a knack for producing delightfully showy, trumpet-shaped flowers—the jacaranda, catalpa, and African tulip trees are good examples. The yellow elder is a deciduous shrub that can reach twenty-five feet high. Each autumn it produces brilliant hanging displays of bell-shaped yellow flowers about two inches long. This is a native of Central America, ranging from southern Arizona to the northern Andes. The name "tecoma" is an abbreviation of the indigenous Mexican name for this shrub, *tecomaxochitl.*

Gerald Carr

# *Euphorbiaceae*

The spurge family has successfully colonized the Earth and largely by thinking small. The flowers are unisexual and typically reduced to near-microscopic size. It's curious, then, that this family gives tropical gardeners several of the most spectacular ornamentals possible. Most of these are grown for their leaf, as opposed to flower, displays. The spurge family also includes two trees of note in Hawai'i—the kukui (the official tree emblem for the State of Hawai'i) and the rubber tree, also the manioc or tapioca plant, with its edible roots, and the castor bean, a garish weed in many parts of the islands.

Breynia disticha 'Roseo-picta'
• **snow bush**

A common hedge plant in Hawai'i, the snow bush throws out fluffy masses of two-inch leaves that are mottled with red, pink, white, and green. Colors are brightest in full sun. Stems are wiry and zigzag. Shrubs are slight, three to six feet tall. Plants propagate easily from cuttings, and the suckers tend to creep into other areas.

## Acalypha hispida • **chenille plant**
## Acalypha wilkesiana • **copper leaf**
## Acalypha wilkesiana 'Godseffiana' • **Jacob's coat**

The copper leaf, a Fiji native, is commonly planted in Hawaiian yards because it needs little pampering and grows rapidly to six to fifteen feet tall. Its attractive leaves are bronze-tinted and spotted with red. The flowers and fruit are obscure, borne on narrow spikes. Leaf color patterns vary widely and freely, and many named varieties exist.

The variety 'Godseffiana' comes from New Guinea and has cream-colored leaf-edges. A different species in the same genus, the chenille plant, is grown for its red, velvety flower spikes that hang to a length of about eighteen inches. As the common name suggests, these spikes look like the tufted cord called chenille that is used for embroidery or fabric fringes. Unlike many other members of the Euphorbiaceae, plants in the genus *Acalypha* are not poisonous. In fact, in some parts of the world the young leaves are cooked and eaten.

*Acalypha wilkesiana,*
*'Godseffiana',* Jacob's coat

*Acalypha hispida,* chenille plant

*Acalypha wilkesiana,* copper leaf

## Codiaeum variegatum • **croton**

The croton bush seems to be in competition with itself to win the "Weird Leaf Award." Different varieties of the same species display markings of red, orange, purple, and yellow in solid, spotted, streaked, and mottled patterns on leaves that range from broad blades to wrinkled ribbons—the variations seem to be unlimited. The original green-leaf form of croton comes from Fiji and the lands west to Australia. The colored-leaf forms are among the most commonly seen yard plants in Hawai'i, partly because they form such robust, thick, dependable shrubbery. They get up to twelve feet tall but are often trimmed as hedges.

## Jatropha, various • **jatropha**

Several members of the genus *Jatropha* are grown in Hawai'i as shrubs or diminutive trees, favored for their bright red or rose flower clusters that burst out of the branch tips. The jatrophas all have milky juice, and the plants, especially the seeds, are poisonous.

**Euphorbia pulcherrima**
# • poinsettia

In colder climates the famous "Christmas flower" of Mexico is widely grown as a rather flimsy potted plant. But in Hawai'i poinsettias make sensational landscape features, forming domes as tall as twelve feet that roar into color from November through March. When the bloom fades, gardeners cut the plants way back to encourage the next season's show. The scarlet form of poinsettia is most common, but you also see white and salmon. The "flowers" are actually colored bracts (modified leaves); the true flowers are rather inconspicuous and green-yellow. Plants are easy to reproduce from cuttings. The milky sap is toxic.

## Euphorbia leucocephala
- **white lace euphorbia**

A close relative of the poinsettia, and also a native of Mexico, the white lace euphorbia or pascuita blooms at the same time as its showy cousin—autumn and winter. It forms a slender shrub up to ten feet tall, with dainty leaves and a cloud of white blossoms. As with poinsettia, it likes good soil and full sun, and its latex sap can irritate the skin.

## Euphorbia cotinifolia
### • fire-on-the-mountain

Another euphorbia, known as red spurge
or fire-on-the-mountain provides color all
year round—the foliage of the entire plant
is purple to blood-red. The more sunlight,
the richer the color. Flowers are insignifi-
cant, small and white. As with its cousins,
this plant produces an irritating milky
juice when its stems are cut or snapped.

89

# Fabaceae

The pea-and-bean family includes many spectacular flowering trees—for example the shower trees, the wiliwili, and the royal Poinciana. These beautiful legumes are featured in our *Tropical Trees of Hawai'i* book. But a couple of their relatives are short enough by nature that Hawai'i's gardeners tend to grow them as shrubs and hedges.

## Calliandra haematocephala
### • pink powderpuff

The Hawaiian name for this showy blossom is "lehua haole" (foreign lehua) because this all-stamen flower resembles that of the native tree 'ōhi'a lehua. (The two plants are not related. 'Ōhi'a lehua is part of the myrtle family, along with guava, bottlebrush, and eucalyptus.) The "powderpuffs" of this Bolivia native measure almost four inches across, and they spangle the foliage throughout the summer and fall. Occasionally you will find a white-flowered form of this species.

90

## Senna alata • **candle bush**

Like candle flames, golden plumes thrust upward from the tips of this woody shrub. Candle bush grows vigorously to eight or even twelve feet tall, but it is short-lived. Flowers persist from spring to fall. The leaves, more than a foot long, are subdivided into pairs of leaflets, sometimes sixteen or more pairs per leaf. The fruit is a typical "beanpod," flat, leathery, and packed with dozens of hard seeds that sprout freely wherever they fall.

# *Liliaceae*

Aloe barbadensis • **true aloe**
Aloe arborescens • **candelabra plant**

The aloes—half onion, half Joshua tree—thrust up their striking flower spikes like saluting swords. These succulent lilies evolved in the African desert. The leaves of the "true" aloe, *Aloe barbadensis*, give off a viscous sap that has relieved many a sunburn. *Aloe arborescens* forms a trunk that can get ten feet high; it throws out its scarlet-orange display during the winter.

IHP Archive

*Aloe barbadensis*, true aloe

*Aloe arborescens*, candelabra plant

Pam Shingaki

# *Lythraceae*

**Cuphea hyssopifolia** • **false heather**

This tough little shrub from Mexico and Guatemala grows less than two feet high. Gardeners plant it along edges and borders. Tiny leaves crowd the furry stems. The tubular flowers, just a quarter-inch long, form at the leaf bases. These flowers—white but turning purple at the throat—sprinkle the plant most of the year.

## Cuphea ignea • **cigar flower**

The cigar flower is a spreading, twiggy, tight-leafed shrub that gets only thigh-high. It produces a ceaseless abundance of tube-shaped red flowers about an inch long. The common name is a witty reference to the fact that the flower's tip is ash-colored. Hawaiians started cultivating this plant in the mid-nineteenth century as a lei flower. The making of such a lei is a lot of work. Flowers aren't strung down the center of the tube, they're speared across the middle.

# *Malpighiaceae*     Galphimia glauca

This head-high shrub from Mexico and Central America spends most of the year producing clusters of bright yellow flowers. The long red stamens add a dash of contrast to the floral display. Leaves come in pairs, pointed at each end, about two inches long. Stems are light gray and brittle. The fruit is a small three-lobed capsule. You might wonder how botanists come up with so many botanical names. In this case, the genus name *Galphimia* is a scramble of the family name, "malpighia."

# *Malvaceae*   Hibiscus, various • **hibiscus**

The flowers of hibiscus—"single flowers," that is (as opposed to the so-called "double flowers," which have multiple petals crowded into a rose-like blossom)—exhibit the unique look of the mallow family, or Malvaceae. Five separate petals fan open behind a single thrusting spike, as the stamens fuse into a tight sheath around the long pistil. This family includes the hollyhock, cotton, okra, the marshmallow (whose root provides a confectioners' ingredient), and one of old Hawai'i's most useful trees, the hau.

The hibiscus has become the floral signature of Hawai'i. Over thirty-three varieties have been brought from afar and crossed with Hawai'i's endemic species to produce thousands of varieties. Horticultural interest in this flower became so feverish that a Hawaiian hibiscus society was formed in 1911, and in 1923 the Territory of Hawai'i passed a law declaring hibiscus to be the official flower.

96

**Hibiscus schizopetalus**

- **coral plant,
  aloalo koʻakoʻa**

A light, graceful shrub from east Africa, this unusual type of hibiscus bears hundreds of hanging red flowers. The petals are finely divided into frills, and they curl back dramatically, exposing the long red staminal column with its curving tip. Horticulturists attempting to breed new hibiscus varieties frequently turn to the pollen of this species.

## Malvaviscus arboreus

- **Turks cap**

Close relative to the true hibiscus, Turks
cap is a tall shrub of the American tropics
that bears a dazzling display of bright
scarlet flowers. Unlike the hibiscus, these
flowers remain closed, with petals furled
into a narrow tube. The staminal column
protrudes a bit from the tip of the flower.

# *Melastomataceae*  Medinilla magnifica • **medinilla**

This gracious shrub from the Philippines has an orchid-like quality, in that it prefers moist, partly-shaded conditions and produces an intricate flower in similar hues. Leaves with bold white veins grow up to a foot long on sharply four-angled stems. Medinilla flowers hang in a cone-shaped cluster, with showy pink bracts up to four inches long flaring above.

# *Ochnaceae*   Ochna kirkii • **Mickey Mouse plant**

No self-respecting shrub should have to bear the name "Mickey Mouse plant." But the bright, fleshy fruits of *Ochna kirkii*—with black seed cases poking like ears out of a red receptacle—remind people of the cartoon character. In habit, the plant looks like a very compact camellia (a relative), the leaves leathery and shiny. The spring flowers are yellow, like buttercups. In light shade, which it prefers, this bush will grow to twelve feet tall.

# *Onagraceae*   Fuchsia magellanica • **fuchsia**

The lovely fuchsia flower of the potted-plant trade has also made its stand in Hawai'i, where in damp, shady areas it grows into a shrub sometimes six feet tall. It has also escaped into wet forests on Hawai'i island, Maui, and Kaua'i. There are many hybrids of this hardy plant from southern South America. The Hawaiian name, kulapepeiao, means "earring"—a term suggested by the way these flowers dangle on their stems.

# Plumbaginaceae   Plumbago auriculata • **plumbago**

A South African native, plumbago is widely grown in warm regions as a shrub or hedge that produces pleasant powder-blue (or white) flowers nearly all year long. Its natural habit is to sprawl and climb over the landscape, assimilating itself with little care.

# Rubiaceae

Rubiaceae is one of the largest families of flowering plants, most of them tropical. It includes coffee and quinine, many types of indigenous Hawaiian plants, and the noni (*Morinda citrifolia*), which was brought to the islands by the ancient Polynesians for its medicinal qualities. The family also includes some show-pieces of the Hawaiian garden.

*Gardenia jasminoides*, gardenia

## Gardenia jasminoides • **gardenia**
## Gardenia taitensis • **tiare**

A native of China, gardenia is grown around the world, even grown under glass, for the pleasure of inhaling the fragrance of its large waxy white flowers. Gardenias thrive in Hawai'i, growing into vigorous shrubs up to six feet high. The flowers, usually with multiple petals like hybrid roses, are strung into the choicest lei. A similar shrub from Tahiti, the tiare, bears a simpler flower with five or more petals in a pinwheel. Tiare is also hauntingly fragrant.

OPPOSITE PAGE:
*Gardenia taitensis*, tiare

# Mussaenda erythrophylla · **Ashanti blood**

This coffee relative from West Africa grows as tall as thirty feet. When it blooms, the puffy heaps of rose-colored bracts seem to overpower the shrub and its tiny flowers.

## Coffea arabica · **coffee**

Coffee plants came to Hawai'i in 1823, first planted in Manoa Valley, O'ahu. Now it is grown on all the islands, but it favors the Kona district because this region routinely gets afternoon clouds. Although it grows as small trees, reaching fifteen feet high on slender, flexible trunks, coffee thinks of itself as an understory plant—it likes protection from intense sunlight. The cascades of white flowers are known as "Hawaiian snow." The subsequent sight of the red "cherries" against shiny dark-green foliage is quite attractive.

## Ixora coccinea · **ixora**

Ixora is one of the most widely planted landscaping shrubs in Hawai'i's coastal areas. Its popularity is partly due to this plant's compact growth habit, staying to four feet or less. Also, given adequate water, ixora tolerates heat and harsh exposure. But the real pay-off with ixora is its generosity of bloom. It never stops covering itself with vivid domes of uniformly coral-red blossoms, each cluster about eight inches across. These make good cut flowers, and individual flowers can be strung into lei.

# *Rutaceae* — Murraya paniculata • **mock orange**

A shrub with thick, rich foliage and sweet-smelling white flowers in summer and fall, mock orange is popular in many warm-climate regions. In some situations it can get tree-like, but usually you see it trimmed as a hedge no higher than six or eight feet. This is a citrus relative (the common name is somewhat accurate), although its half-inch red berries are not to be eaten. A native of India and East Asia, this plant's small leaflets—three to seven to a leaf—stand up well to shaping and topiary work.

IHP Archive

# *Scrophulariaceae*

This bright-flowered family includes the snapdragon, the foxglove, and the Indian paintbrush. Typically, its four thousand species are soft-tissue annuals or perennials of temperate regions. Flowers tend to be tubular or bell-shaped with an irregular design.

## Russelia equisetiformis • **firecracker plant**

This droopy shrub, which grows no more than four feet high, rarely forms leaves. Instead, its wispy stems do the work of photosynthesis. The inch-long, tubular flowers, red as firecrackers, bloom abundantly all year round. Hawai'i's landscapers use this plant as a color accent, a deep groundcover, or a low hedge. Native to Mexico, firecracker plant (also called coral plant) requires little care and water, but it does prefer some shade from direct sunlight.

# Solanaceae

Solanaceae is a widely distributed and quite diverse family that provides us with the tomatoes, potatoes, peppers, eggplants, and a wide variety of toxic and medicinal plants, including tobacco.

## Brugmansia candida • **angel's trumpet, nānāhonua**

The Hawaiian name means "gazing downward," a nice term for the flowering habit of this prolific bloomer. Trumpet-shaped flowers about ten inches long—white or apricot-colored—hang and swing in the breeze. This is a tall, fast-growing shrub, very loose and open in form with thin, brittle branches. Leaves are large, a foot or more long, pale green and fuzzy. The whole plant has a musky scent, and all parts are toxic. These plants were brought to Hawai'i from South America as early as 1825.

## Brunfelsia pauciflora • **yesterday-today-and-tomorrow**

This compact, smooth-leafed shrub gets four to six feet tall. At least twice a year it will surge into blossom, turning itself into a globe of color—of colors, plural, rather, because these flowers open a deep lavender and fade quickly to light lavender, then white. (This speedy color change inspires the common name.) The entire display lasts just a few weeks, but it's a welcome sight whenever it returns. Flowers are about an inch across and sweetly fragrant. A native of Brazil, this type of brunfelsia is easy to grow in full sun, requiring little more than ample water.

## Capsicum annuum
## • red pepper, nīoi

The fruit of the pepper plant—with its many shapes, colors, and degrees of fiery intensity—plays a role in almost all human cultures and cuisines. Starting in about 1815, the Hawaiians adopted this spice for their otherwise bland cuisine. The classic Hawaiian chili pepper is a narrow, cone-shaped fruit just one inch long, bright red, and blisteringly hot. Typically, the islanders will drop a few peppers into a jar of fresh water and let them sit for a few days. A splash of this "chili water" is more than enough to spice a stew or a slab of sashimi.

### Streptosolen jamesonii
### • **marmalade bush**

A sun-loving shrub from Colombia and
Ecuador, the marmalade bush grows
about six feet tall with long, rambling
branches that like to interweave with
neighboring plants. The common name
refers to the rich orange-to-red color of
the flowers, which cluster at the end of
each branch. The dark, shiny leaves are
oval, about an inch long, and creased
with deep veins. The plain, five-petaled
corolla flairs out from a narrow, twisted,
inch-long tube.

# *Verbenaceae*    Duranta repens • **golden dewdrop**

The name comes from the bright golden berries that hang in clusters much of the year. The weight of their treasure tends to burden the stems. Flowers are small, light lavender blue, and arrayed in loose clusters at the branch tips. Each flower is a small tube flaring into five lobes. Makes a good informal hedge or screen from six to eighteen feet high.

## *Holmskioldia sanguinea*

- **Chinaman's hat, cup-and-saucer**

Native to the Himalayas, this eight-foot-tall shrub is popular for its odd flowers, which look something like satellite dishes. A plate-like calyx of red or orange surrounds a spike-like red flower that protrudes from the center. Lei-makers like to use these floral gems in the long-lasting braided arrangements called haku lei. Oval, pointed leaves up to four inches long grow in pairs opposite one another. It's possible to find a yellow-flowering variation of this plant.

# Garden Vines

Why is it that so many
vines bear spectacular
blossoms? Perhaps it's just
to keep gardeners smiling
while the plants attempt to
smother everything
in the yard.

# *Acanthaceae*   Thunbergia alata · **black-eyed Susan**

The genus *Thunbergia* includes many showy bloomers. Flowers are typically funnel- or bell-shaped with five similar lobes. The black-eyed Susan is a popular annual in cold climates. In Hawai'i it persists year to year, aggressively covering whole hillsides with generous displays of orange or yellow flowers, each with a dark purple throat. This native of Africa is widely naturalized in tropical regions. The sky flower or blue trumpet vine, from India, has flaring, five-inch flowers of the color suggested by its names. This vine is so vigorous that you should keep it out of the garden, unless you want a fight on your hands.

# *Apocynaceae*

Allamanda cathartica • **allamanda**

Mandevilla, various • **pink mandevilla**

Two plants of the dogbane family are common color-spots in the Hawaiian garden. See also their native cousin, the maile vine (page 21). The yellow allamanda is a sturdy, robust vine with firm, shiny leaves of medium green. This is a profuse, continuous bloomer. Allamanda can climb to heights of fifty feet or cover banks. But they are fairly easy to control by trimming, and you sometimes see them contained into mounded shrubs. The pink mandevilla is by its nature far more restrained. A twining vine, it needs a trellis or fence for support and rich, well-watered soil. The reward for care is its summer display of large pink bell-shaped flowers.

*Allamanda cathartica*, allamanda

*Mandevilla spp*, pink mandevilla

# *Asclepiadaceae*   Hoya carnosa • **wax vine**

The milkweed family (see crown flower, page 81), gives us three very desirable flowering vines. The wax vine derives its name from the unusual density of its delicate flowers. If a candlemaker wanted to turn jeweler, he might carve something like these fragrant pink-and-white sculptures arranged in half-sphere sprays. The leaves, too, are thick and well-made. Perhaps because such work takes a lot of care, this vine is rather delicate and slight, needs support, and prefers growing in sheltered shady areas.

Gordon Daida

### Stephanotis floribunda
- ## stephanotis, bridal bouquet

Stephanotis is more robust and does well in full sun in Hawai'i's humid regions. Like the wax vine, though, it has thick leaves and dense flowers. The fragrance of these pure-white sprays is enchanting. In Hawai'i stephanotis flowers are traditionally worn by brides. Wax vine originates in China and Australia; stephanotis comes from Madagascar.

### Telosma cordata
- ## Chinese violet, pakalana

Say "pakalana" and people think "perfume." This native of India and China produces a popular lei flower—popular not for the glamour of its flowers, which are yellow-green about a half inch long, but for the delight of its fragrance. The flimsy heart-shaped leaves, up to four inches long, stand on long stems away from the furry, wire-like branches.

Veronica Carmona

# *Bignoniaceae*  Pandorea jasminoides • **bower plant**

This fast-growing climber from Australia is grown for its showy pink (sometimes white) flowers. The glossy leaves divide into pairs of narrow leaflets arranged along a long midrib. The flowers are two-inch-long trumpets with dark-pink veins emphasizing the flairing throats. This is a common roadside plant in parts of Hawai'i.

## Pyrostegia ignea • **orange trumpet, huapala**

Huapala picks the unlikely month of January to let loose its cascade of flaming orange flowers. Each flower is a slender tube two to three inches long formed of five fused petals, three of them curling back at the tips and two that hold together as a kind of landing spot for insect pollinators. Older flowers slip from their calyx and hang for a while, dangling from the long pistil. Foliage is glossy bright green. For some reason, old-timers say that planting huapala near the front door puts a curse on romance.

# *Cactaceae*   Hylocereus undatus • **night-blooming cereus**

The term "cactus" is not generally associated with the idea of tree-climbing vines, but the night-blooming cereus answers to both labels. This oddity's fleshy, three-winged stems produce aerial roots that help it clamber up walls and trees. During the summer and fall it issues great displays of foot-long, yellow-white flowers that open in the early evening, emit a spicy fragrance, then wither the next morning. The first night-blooming cereus came to Honolulu in 1830 aboard the brig *Ivanhoe*. Hawai'i's best-known planting is a quarter-mile hedge located on the campus of Punahou School.

Veronica Carmona

# *Convolvulaceae*  Ipomoea horsfalliae • **Prince Kūhiō vine**

This vine produces attention-grabbing masses of magenta-crimson flowers in fall and winter. The waxy flowers are bell-shaped with a long throat and a wide-flaring mouth of five lobes. The leaves fan like five fingers attached at the same point. Prince Kūhiō, Hawai'i's first elected territorial representative to U.S. Congress, brought this Brazilian native to the islands. For many years a large specimen grew over his Waikīkī house. This tall, branching wine will climb as high as thirty feet.

Gordon Daida

## Merremia tuberosa • **wood rose**

The wood rose is not a rose, of course—rather, it is a yellow-flowering type of morning glory (see page 26) with large, deeply lobed leaves. The unique seed capsules look something like flowers carved out of translucent wood and are often used in dried arrangements. Native to tropical America, the wood rose is now common throughout the tropics. In Hawai'i it sometimes escapes in disturbed areas.

# *Fabaceae*   Canavalia cathartica • **Mauna Loa vine**

A typical vine of the pea-and-bean family, the "Mauna Loa" vine likes to clamber around in waste places on its tough wiry stems. Each papery dull-green leaf is composed of three triangular leaflets. The showy pink-lavender flowers follow the classic pea design, with three petals thrown back and two fused to form a protective "keel" around the developing legume pod. This rather weedy plant from Madagascar became a Hawai'i icon when lei-makers invented the classic mauna loa lei, a flat ribbon of pink made by meticulously stringing pairs of these flowers then folding together individual petals.

Veronica Carmona

## Strongylodon macrobotrys • **jade vine**

The jade vine is a strange variation on the basic formula of the pea-and-bean family. The blue-green blossoms hang in panicles up to three feet long. A native of the Philippines, this plant is by nature an aggressive climber that likes to establish itself thickly overhead so that it can shade its own roots and drop its blossoms into the sheltered space beneath. It's an excellent choice for arbors and pergolas. Flowers are commonly strung into lei.

# *Nyctaginaceae* Bougainvillea, various • **bougainvillea**

These Brazil natives are popular everywhere they thrive—which is any hot,
dry, frost-free climate. Bougainvillea is a
standard landscape feature of Hawai'i's
leeward beach communities. Plants need
little water, love the sun, and give off
endless displays of brilliant red, purple,
or orange. (One rarity is even white.)
As with many showy plants, the color
actually comes not from the relatively
obscure flowers but from the large,
papery bracts that enclose them.
Gardeners beware: this is an extremely
robust, woody plant armed with vicious
thorns, and it likes to spread out. Any
attempt to raise them in tidy confinement
is self-defeating. Bougainvillea is a plant
best appreciated from a distance.

# Oleaceae   Jasminum sambac • **pīkake**

The olive family includes plants as diverse as the olive, the ash, privets, and star jasmine. The pīkake, a kind of jasmine, is one of the most favored lei-flower plants. The name "pīkake" (from peacock) derives from the fact that Princess Ka'iulani loved the birds and these flowers equally. The plants are climbing shrubs with round, downy leaves. The white flowers, about an inch across, come in three forms—single, double (literally two flowers that grow together), and rose (one flower with multiple petals). The perfume of these flowers is extraordinary. In its native India, pīkake figures into mythology. In China it flavors tea. It is the national flower of the Philippines.

# Passifloraceae   Passiflora edulis • **liliko'i**

Cat Sweeney

The viny family of the passion flowers originates in the New World. At least eleven species have been brought to Hawai'i for their odd flowers or fruit and have escaped into the wild. Some are at risk of becoming great pests. Here we show the species that produces a prized and tangy edible fruit, called in Hawai'i "liliko'i." There are two varieties, one with a purple rind and one yellow. The pulp is a bright orange slime that clings to crunchy black seeds. The plants climb to great heights (or lengths), grabbing hold with tight-wrapping tendrils. Spaniards discovered the passion flower when they conquered its native land, Latin America. The conquistadors imagined that the elaborate flower structure was emblematic of the passion of Christ—hence the rather unromantic source of its common name.

# *Polygonaceae*   Antigonon leptopus • **Mexican creeper, chain-of-love**

IHP Archive

This wild-looking vine from Mexico assimilates itself easily into the natural landscape, especially dry hot places, scrambling forty feet or more over walls, banks, and trees. Its charming feature is its flower—loose sprays of small pink blooms that the plant throws out everywhere and through most of the year.

# *Solanaceae*   Solandra maxima • **cup of gold**

This fast-growing vine from Mexico, with its big handsome foliage, likes humid places. By nature it's a jungle scrambler. The common name refers to its flowers, of course—big nine-inch goblets that unfurl yellow, sweet-smelling, and streaked with purple, then turn more golden as they age. Some flowers appear all year round, but the peak blooming season is winter. This is an off-beat member of the tomato family, probably a near relation to the angel's trumpet (page 109).

# Crop Flowers

Many of the plants featured
elsewhere in this book as
garden plants also make up
a lively part of the plant-
selling economy of Hawai'i.
Besides the ones shown in
this section, island farmers
also raise carnations, tea
roses, and chrysanthemums.

# "Tropicals"

*Strelitzia reginae*, bird of paradise

*Phaeomeria magnifica*, torch ginger

heliconia

# Proteas

Plants of the family Proteaceae produce extremely showy flowers that last weeks in a vase and then hold their form for use in dry arrangements. The sturdiness of these flowers reflects their native habitat—dry, windswept mountains in South Africa and similar tropical climates, notably Australia. The complex blossom is actually a massive cluster of individual flowers, each one reduced to little more than brightly colored stamens and pistils. Members of the genus *Protea* wrap these blossoms in petal-like bracts. The *Leucospermum* flower is a spherical "pincushion." Plants in the genus *Leucadendron* produce colorful leaf-arrangements at the stem-ends. *Banksia* is an Australian genus that mounts its pincushion-type flowers on heavy cylindrical or cone-shaped receptacles.

*Protea 'King'*

*Pincushion*

*Banksia*

*Leucadendron*

*Protea*

# Plumeria

Plumeria trees are grown commercially for the lei trade, as these plump, sweet-smelling, easy-to-string blooms are deservedly the most popular of lei flowers. Four species of the genus *Plumeria*, all natives of tropical America, produce flowers that range in hue from white with a yellow throat (the "Singapore" variety) through rose and red to a deep wine color. These are short, broad-crowned trees with large, heavy oblong leaves that fall from the tree each winter. Plumerias are also extremely popular features of home gardens and are traditionally planted in cemeteries. (One old common name for them is "make-man flower"—dead man flower.) Plants have a latex sap that oozes freely when the flowers are picked. They grow easily, if rather slowly, from cuttings.

# Sugar Cane

The giant grass named *Saccharum officinarum* is the source of half the world's sugar. It first came to Hawai'i with the early Polynesians, who called it "kō" and had names for forty different varieties. The first commercial cane plantings in the islands started in 1835 in Kōloa, Kaua'i. By the end of that century the sugar industry had established itself as the "king" in Hawai'i. By the end of the twentieth century, the industry had seriously declined, plagued by high land values, high labor costs, and the inability to compete with cheap sugar from other parts of the world. But the culture of sugar, particularly represented by the plantation camps that brought together laborers from many lands, made Hawai'i what it is today. Plants are grown for two years, then harvested (usually before they bloom) by burning then slashing. The canes are crushed in a mill, the sweet juice then cooked.

# *Pineapple*

Pineapple is actually a bromeliad, relative to the bristly, weird-flowered ornamentals illustrated on page 60. *Ananas comosus* is the scientific name; hala kahiki the Hawaiian. The first plants came to the islands only thirty-five years after Cook's discovery. During the 1850s they were grown in Kailua-Kona and traded to whalers. But these early pineapples were inferior to the kind grown exclusively in Hawai'i today—the "Smooth Cayenne," introduced about 1885. By the middle of the twentieth century, Hawai'i was growing 80 percent of the world supply and exporting some forty million cases of canned fruit each year. The plant likes higher altitudes and drier conditions than does sugar cane. After two years in the field, generally in late summer, each plant produces one fruit. Pineapples are easily reproduced by planting cuttings or the top-crowns of the fruit.

# Where to See Hawai'i's Plants

A good way to get close to many of the plants illustrated in this book is to walk around the grounds of Hawai'i's excellent resort hotels. The resorts pride themselves as much on their landscaping as they do on their art collections, waterfalls, and chefs. Many provide signs that identify their in-garden residents.

Go for a drive. On Maui, drive the road to Hāna for an intense experience of rainforest exuberance, or drive up to 'Īao Valley and the state park. On Hawai'i, you can tool around Hilo and its outskirts for the same effect; make sure you include the state park at 'Akaka Falls. On Kaua'i, drive through Hanalei to the road's end at Hā'ena. If you're in Honolulu, explore the city and its neighborhoods, so botanically rich.

If you want to get yourself off the roadway and walk or hike into uninhabited, wild Hawai'i, use the professional hiking guides—human or literary—that are available on all islands. The Nature Conservancy of Hawai'i offers some

'Īao Valley

opportunities to explore a few remaining pockets of the primordial landscape.

And of course Hawai'i has wonderful botanical gardens on all the major islands.

The National Tropical Botanical Garden is the only national, privately supported botanical garden chartered by the U.S. Congress. It manages three gardens on Kaua'i and one on Maui. The Kaua'i sites

include two right next to each other in a hidden-away valley in the south—Lāwa'i, the former vacation home of Queen Emma, wife of Kamehameha IV. Allerton Garden features some brilliantly designed landscape elements, and McBryde Gardens is a 252-acre scientific research center. Access is available by tours only on given days, so call first. At the extreme opposite north end of Kaua'i, Limahuli Gardens is doing amazing work to restore the original native landscape.

You can drop into Limahuli for a self-guided walk most days of the week.

On Maui, the National Tropical Botanical Garden site lies close to the town of Hāna. This is Kahanu Garden, which includes the largest heiau (ancient Hawaiian temple) in the state. You have to call them to schedule a tour. Maui has other fine gardens open to the public for a modest admission fee—including the Kula Botanical Gardens and the Enchanting Floral Gardens, both in Kula. Maui Tropical Plantation has beautiful plants with a tram tour that emphasizes food plants of the tropics.

On the "Big Island," Hawai'i, visit two botanical gardens in the Hilo area. Hawai'i Tropical Botanical Gardens is a wild, wet place on the Hāmākua Coast north of the city. Nani Maui Gardens, closer to town, has theme gardens laid out over twenty acres.

In downtown Honolulu (right near Chinatown) visit Foster Garden, which

people love for the beauty of its huge, rare trees. If you're on the North Shore, go to Waimea Valley Audubon Center, which offers the possibility of botanizing to those who consider the discovery of plants a valid kind of adventure.

'Akaka Falls

# Paul Wood

Paul Wood had the fortune in youth to apprentice with an extraordinary naturalist—Oscar C. Clarke, long-time curator of the herbarium at University of California Riverside. He worked as Oscar Clarke's herbarium assistant, then carried his passion for botany into a couple of mid-twenties gigs—as a nurseryman (California certified) and as a landscape contractor. In time, he got re-focused on his abiding work as a writer and writing teacher. Now, after twenty-five years in Hawai'i, this book along with others titles, *Tropical Trees of Hawai'i* and *Proteas*, has given him the opportunity to pull a few threads together.

# Ron Dahlquist

Ron Dahlquist sold his first picture to a small surfing publication almost thirty years ago. Today he is a nationally acclaimed photographer whose repertoire ranges from action sports to sensitive pictures of the environment and worldwide travel. His images have appeared in such publications as *Life, Time, National Geographic, World, Forbes, Esquire, Islands, Condé Nast Traveler, Vanity Fair, Outside, Ski, Surfer's Journal, Snowboarder,* and *Windsurfer.* His coffee table book *Under a Maui Sun* was released at the end of 2000. A Maui resident, he has long held a photographer's fascination for the design and color of Hawai'i's blossoms and trees as evident in his work in *Proteas* and *Tropical Trees of Hawai'i.*

**'a'ali'i • 37**
Dodonea viscosa

**allamanda • 117**
Allamanda cathartica

**amaryllis • 55**
Hippeastrum puniceum
Barbados lily

**angel's trumpet • 109**
Brugmansia candida
nānāhonua

**anthurium • 57**
Anthurium, various

**Ashanti blood • 104**
Mussaenda erythrophylla

**'awa • 36**
Piper methysticum
kava

**banana • 35**
Musa x paradisiaca
mai'a

**beach morning glory • 26**
Ipomoea pes-capraea
pōhuehue

**beach naupaka • 30**
Scaevola sericea
naupaka kahakai

**bird of paradise • 70**
Strelitzia reginae

**black-eyed Susan • 116**
Thunbergia alata

**blue ginger • 63**
Dichorisandra thyrsiflora

**bougainvillea • 127**
Bougainvillea, various

**bower plant • 120**
Pandorea jasminoides

**Brazilian plume flower • 77**
Justicia carnea

**bromeliads • 60**
Bromeliads, various

**candelabra plant • 92**
Aloe arborescens

**candle bush • 91**
Senna alata

**canna • 61**
Canna indica
ali'ipoe

chenille plant • 84
Acalypha hispida

Chinaman's hat • 113
Holmskioldia sanguinea
cup-and-saucer

Chinese violet • 119
Telosma cordata
pakalana

cigar flower • 94
Cuphea ignea

coffee • 105
Coffea arabica

coleus • 64
Plectranthus scutellarioides

copper leaf • 84
Acalypha wilkesiana

coral plant • 97
Hibiscus schizopetalus
aloalo ko'ako'a

croton • 85
Codiaeum variegatum

crown flower • 81
Calotropis gigantea

cup of gold • 130
Solandra maxima

eldorado • 78
Pseuderanthemum
reticulatum

elephant's ear • 22
Alocasia macrorrhiza
'ape

evening primrose • 45
Oenothera spp

false heather • 93
Cuphea hyssopifolia

firecracker plant • 106
Russelia equisetiformis

fire-on-the-mountain • 89
Euphorbia cotinifolia

fuchsia • 100
Fuchsia magellanica

Galphimia glauca • 95

gardenia • 102
Gardenia jasminoides

**giant bird of paradise • 72**
Strelitzia nicolai

**gingers • 50**
Gingers, various

**glory bush • 44**
Tibouchina urvilleana

**golden dewdrop • 112**
Duranta repens

**heliconia • 43**
Heliconia, various

**hibiscus • 33**
Hibiscus, various
aloalo

**hibiscus • 96**
Hibiscus cultivars

**'ilima • 34**
Sida fallax

**impatiens • 58**
Impatiens wallerana

**ixora • 105**
Ixora coccinea

**Jacob's coat • 84**
Acalypha wilkesiana
'Godseffiana'

**jade vine • 124**
Strongylodon macrobotrys

**jatropha • 86**
Jatropha, various

**Job's tears • 48**
Coix lachryma-jobi
pū'ohe'ohe

**lantana • 49**
Lantana camara

**liliko'i • 128**
Passiflora edulis

**maile • 21**
Alyxia oliviformis

**marmalade bush • 111**
Streptosolen jamesonii

**Mauna Loa vine • 124**
Canavalia cathartica

**medinilla • 99**
Medinilla magnifica

**Mexican creeper • 130**
Antigonon leptopus
chain-of-love

**Mickey Mouse plant • 100**
Ochna kirkii

**mock orange • 106**
Murraya paniculata

**montbretia • 64**
Crocosmia x crocosmiflora

**morning glory • 26**
Ipomoea, various
koali

**night-blooming cereus • 122**
Hylocereus undatus

**'ōhelo • 29**
Vaccinium reticulatum

**oleander • 80**
Nerium oleander

**orange trumpet • 120**
Pyrostegia ignea
huapala

**orchids • 67**
various

**pīkake • 128**
Jasminum sambac

**pineapple • 141**
Ananas comosus
hala kahiki

**pink mandevilla • 117**
Mandevilla, various

**pink powderpuff • 90**
Calliandra haematocephala

**plumbago • 101**
Plumbago auriculata

**plumeria • 139**
Plumeria, various

**poinsettia • 87**
Euphorbia pulcherrima

**prickly pear • 42**
Opuntia ficus-indica
pānini

**prickly poppy • 47**
Argemone glauca
pua kala

**Prince Kūhiō vine • 123**
Ipomoea horsfalliae